MY HAPPY EARS

Written By: NaTyshca Pickett

Illustrated By Ishika Sharma

I dedicate this book to God for making this all possible, thank you for the vision. To Brandon, you are an amazing father and I couldn't do this without you. To Desmond for being an awesome big brother, helper and wonderful son and to Adrion, you are the definition of joy. Thank you for teaching us the true meaning of happiness.

With Love,

Your wife and mom

MY HAPPY EARS

My name is Adrion and I am four years old. When I was born, the doctors said that I will have to live with hearing loss.

I have conductive hearing loss in both of my ears. That means that some of my bones in my middle ear did not grow all the way.

Just because I have hearing loss does not mean that I do not have fun. With my hearing aids, I have happy ears.

I also like being with my mommy, daddy and brother Desmond.

When I am not wearing my hearing aids I feel left out and it can be hard for me to hear what others are saying.

Desmond makes sure that I am not left out and will give me my hearing aids when he sees that I have taken them off.

With my hearing aids, I can hear all kinds of sounds around me. I like when my dad reads the paper to me. It helps me learn new words.

One day, mommy and daddy tell me that I am going to start a new school.

I tell Desmond that I do not want to go to school. I think the kids will laugh at me because I wear hearing aids.

Desmond tells me not to worry, because my hearing aids are cool and I'm fun to be around.

After talking to Desmond, I feel better and ready to start my new school.

The next day, daddy and I walk to my new classroom. I get nervous and ask daddy to come inside with me.

I see other kids who are going into my classroom and they say hi to me.

They also wear hearing aids just like me.

I wave goodbye to daddy because I am not scared anymore. I am ready to start my new school where the students have happy ears just like me.

THE END

Acknowledgements

To my Mother in Love, Felicia, you are awesome beyond words and have always been here in the trenches with us every step of the way, we can't thank you enough and we love you. Mikey, you are the best uncle the boys can have. They love their Uncle Mikey and we appreciate you!

To our Hood, Pickett and Smith families, your support is beyond amazing , we love you and thank you.

To our close friends we appreciate you for support and sharing our book with everyone you know.

To Desert Voices Oral Learning staff, your dedication and hard work for our Adrion does not go unnoticed. You are an extension of our family and we appreciate everything you do day in and day our for the Deaf and Hard of Hearing Community. You all are amazing!

Made in the USA
Las Vegas, NV
25 August 2021